Common Core Lessons & Activities:
Chemical Reactions

By Carole Marsh
Published by Gallopade International, Inc.

Printed in the U.S.A. (Peachtree City, Georgia)

TABLE OF CONTENTS

G: Includes Graphic Organizer
GO: Graphic Organizer is also available 8½" x 11" online
download at www.gallopade.com/client/go
(numbers above correspond to the graphic organizer numbers online)

Why Study Chemistry?

Read the text and answer the questions.

When I found out I had to take a chemistry class this year, I wasn't happy. Immediately, I imagined complicated equations and boring lectures. I also figured I'd have to perform difficult experiments that had no connection to my everyday life. Boy, was I wrong!

Actually, chemistry class is nothing like I thought it would be! The most interesting thing I have learned is that chemistry happens every day in the world around us—and even in our own bodies!

How would I describe chemistry to a new student? I'd say chemistry is studying matter and how it changes. What is matter? Matter is everything that has mass and takes up space. Matter is everything we can use or touch. And all matter is made of chemicals!

I've learned that we use chemistry every day. When you help make dinner, you use chemistry. When you wash the dishes, you use chemistry. When you take a pill to ease your headache, you use chemistry.

Learning about chemical reactions helps you understand all kinds of things. For example, I know that ingredients in cake batter react to make a light, fluffy cake. I've also learned how mixing certain medicines can cause bad reactions. That's why you need to pay attention to warnings on medicine bottles!

I'm really excited to see what else I learn this year in chemistry. Who knew science could be so much fun?!

1. This text is written in what point of view?
   A. first person   B. second person   C. third person
2. Use information from the text to define chemistry in your own words.
3. Summarize the main idea of the text.
4. Considering that the body is made of chemical elements, infer why medications are effective in the human body.
5. Work in groups. Use online resources to find 5 additional examples of chemistry in everyday life. Compare your examples and discuss.

What is a Chemical Reaction?

Read the text and answer the questions.

Chemical reactions occur when molecules <u>interact</u>. When molecules interact, they can create new molecules. The new molecules have different chemical and physical properties. The substances that interact to create a chemical change are called *reactants*. The substances created with new chemical and physical properties are called *products*.

Chemical reactions occur all the time. In fact, there are <u>infinite</u> combinations of chemical reactions that can occur with the right conditions. Some common examples of chemical reactions are when a cut apple turns brown, metal rusts, and bread molds.

To identify a chemical reaction, it is important to understand the difference between a *physical change* and a *chemical change*. Chemical reactions must always include a chemical change.

A physical change is when a substance changes in appearance only. An example of a physical change is when ice melts. Ice and water have the same chemical properties, but have different physical forms. A chemical change is when the basic makeup of a substance changes. An example of a chemical change is when wood burns. When the carbon in the wood reacts with oxygen in the air, ash and smoke are created. The wood has changed permanently into another form.

1. A. Use a dictionary to define <u>interact</u> as it is used in the text.
   B. Use a dictionary to define <u>infinite</u>. List a synonym and an antonym.
2. A. When wood burns, what are the reactants?
   B. When wood burns, what are the products?
3. A. What is the difference between a physical change and a chemical change?
   B. Which change is required for a chemical reaction?
4. What substance do you think reacts with a cut apple to turn it brown? Compare your answer with classmates and discuss.

Types of Chemical Reactions

Read the text, study the diagrams, and answer the questions.

There are many types of chemical reactions. Some of the most common types are synthesis, decomposition, single displacement, double displacement, and combustion.

Synthesis chemical reactions occur when two different substances combine to create a new substance. An example of a synthesis reaction is when hydrogen and oxygen come together to create a new substance: water. This diagram shows how a synthesis reaction works:

Synthesis Reaction

Decomposition chemical reactions occur when a compound breaks into two different substances. An example of a decomposition reaction is when water, a compound, breaks down into oxygen and hydrogen gas. This diagram shows how a decomposition reaction works:

Decomposition Reaction

A *single displacement* chemical reaction occurs when a more active substance displaces, or removes, a less active substance to form a new compound. An example of a single displacement reaction is when hydrochloric acid and zinc react. Zinc replaces the hydrogen atoms in hydrochloric acid and creates a new single compound: hydrogen. This diagram shows how a single displacement reaction works:

Single Displacement Reaction

A *double displacement* chemical reaction occurs when an element from two different compounds displace each other. In other words, two compounds trade substances. This diagram shows how a double displacement reaction works:

Double Displacement Reaction

Combustion chemical reactions occur when a compound containing carbon combines with oxygen. Combustion reactions produce energy in the form of heat. Common examples of combustion reactions are a lit match or fireworks.

1. Use the text to make a chart to list and describe five common types of chemical reactions.
2. Use online or classroom resources to identify 2 other types of chemical reactions not listed in the text.
3. What type of chemical reaction happens when a compound breaks into two different substances?
4. What type of chemical reaction produces energy in the form of heat?
5. If AB is a compound element that becomes the single substances A and B, what type of chemical reaction occurred? Cite evidence from the text to support your answer.
6. If AB and C react to create AC and B, what type of chemical reaction occurred? Cite evidence from the text to support your answer.
7. A. Water is the product of what type of chemical reaction?
   B. What are the reactants in the chemical reaction that creates water?
8. A. Create your own diagram to show a combustion reaction.
   B. Do diagrams help you understand concepts in chemistry? Explain why or why not.

Signs of Chemical Reactions

Read the text and answer the questions.

In order to determine if a chemical reaction has occurred, chemists look for specific signs. Ways to tell if a chemical reaction has taken place include: *color* change; energy (*heat*) is absorbed or released; *odor* changes; a *gas* is produced; or a *solid* is produced.

Color change: Colorful autumn leaves on trees are an example of a chemical reaction that produces a color change. When the amount of sunlight changes in the fall, leaves absorb less light. This produces a pigment change resulting in the bright colors.

Heat: Energy can be either released (exothermic) or consumed (endothermic) in a chemical reaction. An example of an exothermic reaction is the flame of a candle. An example of an endothermic reaction is when a plant's leaves absorb sunlight during photosynthesis.

Odor: A change in odor is also a sign of a chemical reaction. Smells can be sweet, bitter, pleasant, or unpleasant. The smell of a rotten egg is an example of an odor resulting from a chemical reaction.

Gas: Chemical reactions can produce a gas. Gas is a substance that floats like air and can bubble and expand. The bubbles that form when mixing baking soda and vinegar are an example of a gas formation.

Solid: The formation of a solid, or precipitate, is evidence of a chemical reaction. A precipitate is a solid formed by a chemical reaction in a liquid solution. An example is the soap scum that forms when minerals in hard water react with soap molecules.

1. Summarize the main idea of the text.
2. Create a graphic organizer to list and explain the signs of a chemical reaction.
3. Work in groups. Each group will use online resources to find at least two more examples of each chemical change sign described in the text. Compare your answers and discuss. Which examples have you experienced yourself?

Chemical or Physical Change?

Complete the graphic organizer by identifying whether the process is a physical or chemical change. Explain your answers.

Process	Type of Change	Explanation
Burning leaves		
Fireworks		
Melting ice		
Baking bread		
Car rust		
Moldy bread		
Frying eggs		
Sharpening a pencil		
Boiling water		
Chewing food		

Chemical Reaction Disaster

Read the text, quotes, and news report and answer the questions.

A gas leak at a Union Carbide pesticide plant in Bhopal, India, is cited as one of the chemical industry's greatest tragedies.

On December 3, 1984, methyl isocyanate gas leaked from the facility during the early hours of the morning while local residents slept. About 2,000 people died immediately, with another 8,000 dying later.

The initial investigation said that large volumes of water had entered the chemical tank, which caused a chemical reaction that led to the leak. The incident highlighted the risk of having a chemical plant located near an area with a high population.

The following quotes are from people who experienced the gas leak:

"At about 12:30 a.m. I woke to the sound of Ruby coughing badly. I heard a great noise of people shouting. They were yelling 'bhaago, bhaago' (run, run). Moshin started coughing too and then I started coughing with each breath seeming as if we were breathing in fire..."

–Aziza Sultan, a resident of Bhopal

"We were sleeping, when suddenly my daughter woke us up. She said her eyes were burning. Soon all of us in the family had the same sensation as if someone was burning chilies. We all began coughing. Then, when I opened the window, I saw people running for their lives."

–Harish Singh Yadav, a resident of Bhopal

The following excerpt is from a news account distributed by the British Broadcasting Corporation (BBC) Dec. 3, 1984.

1984: Hundreds die in Bhopal chemical accident

Hundreds of people have died from the effects of toxic gases which leaked from a chemical factory near the central Indian city of Bhopal.

The accident happened in the early hours of this morning at the American-owned Union Carbide Pesticide Plant three miles (4.8 km) from Bhopal.

Mr. Y P Gokhale, managing director of Union Carbide in India said that methyl isocyanate gas (MIC) had escaped when a valve in the plant's underground storage tank broke under pressure.

This caused a deadly cloud of lethal gas to float from the factory of Bhopal, which is home to more than 900,000 people – many of whom live in slums.

Chaos and panic broke out in the city and surrounding areas as tens of thousands of people attempted to escape. More than 20,000 people have required hospital treatment for symptoms including swollen eyes, frothing at the mouth, and breathing difficulties.

1. Use a dictionary to define pesticide. Infer what kind of chemicals are used to make a pesticide.
2. What sign indicated that a chemical reaction had taken place in the Bhopal disaster? Cite evidence from the text to support your answer.
3. A. Identify the first-hand accounts of the event.
   B. Identify the second-hand account of the event.
4. How are the first-hand and second-hand accounts different? How are they similar?
5. What effect do the first-hand accounts have on the reader? How can first-hand accounts be effective in stirring up emotions or vividly describing a situation?
6. What effect does the second-hand account have on the reader? Why are second-hand accounts essential to report information?
7. Infer how the plant's location contributed to the tragedy. Could the results have been different if the plant was located far away from a densely populated area?

Photosynthesis

Read the text and answer the questions.

Did you know that a chemical reaction occurs in plants every day? Photosynthesis is the process plants use to make their own food. Plants don't need to hunt and gather or have a caretaker feed them—they can produce food on their own. The only ingredients they need are sunlight, water, and carbon dioxide.

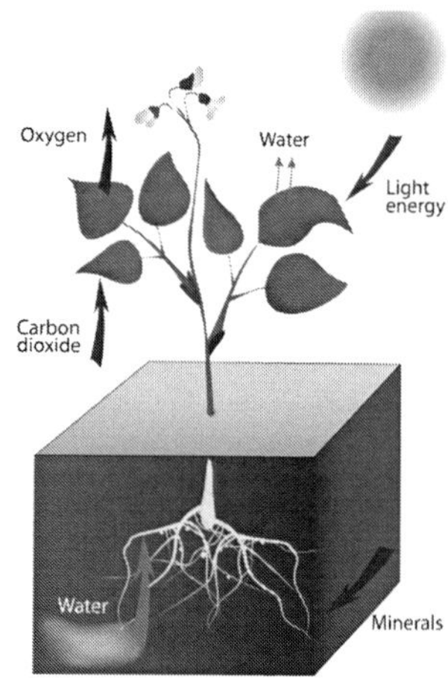

Photosynthesis occurs in the leaves of the plant. A leaf has very small <u>pores</u> called stomata. It also has many cell structures that contain chloroplasts. The chloroplasts have a green chemical inside called chlorophyll. That's why leaves are green! The parts of the leaf work together to complete the photosynthesis process.

First, fresh air flows through the stomata and carbon dioxide enters the leaf. Then, water is absorbed through the stem of the plant and drawn up to the leaf. Finally, the chlorophyll in the leaf absorbs sunlight. The energy from the sunlight splits the water molecules in the leaves into hydrogen and oxygen. The plant doesn't need oxygen, so it releases it back into the air. The leftover hydrogen and carbon dioxide form glucose, or food energy, for the plant. Plants use the "food" to grow. Extra food is stored throughout the plant, in its roots, stems, flowers, fruits, and leaves.

1. Use a dictionary to define <u>pores</u>. List a synonym.
2. "Photo" means light and "synthesis" means putting together. How do the meanings of these words describe the process of photosynthesis?
3. A. List 3 things a plant needs for photosynthesis to occur.
   B. What 2 things are created when photosynthesis occurs?
4. Plants take in carbon dioxide and give off oxygen. What gases do humans take in and exhale when they breathe? Research the answer and explain how plants and humans/animals support each other.

How Soap Works

Read the text and answer the questions.

Nothing is better than a hot shower when you're really dirty. The refreshing water washes off dirt. But it needs a little help—so you pull out the soap and shampoo to clean your body and hair. Did you know that every time you take a shower or wash your clothes chemical reactions are taking place?

Soap is a part of the family of detergents, along with shampoo and laundry detergent. Detergents are chemicals that break up and remove grease and dirt. The most important ingredients in detergents are surfactants. A surfactant helps water wash better. On its own, water forms into droplets and does not cover surfaces well. Surfactants allow water to spread farther and get deep into dirty surfaces.

Surfactants also have another special feature. One side of the molecule repels water and attracts dirt while another side of the molecule attracts water and repels dirt. The result is that surfactants gather dirt with one end and wash it away with another.

One example of a surfactant at work is laundry detergent cleaning clothes. The surfactants in laundry detergent make water wetter and allow it to mix with oil and grease. The surfactants attract dirt to lift it from the clothes, then wash it away.

Shampoo is another detergent that uses surfactants. Shampoo rids hair of naturally forming grease called sebum. In shampoo, the surfactants attract grease and grime and wash it away with water.

1. The word surfactant is a combination of the words "surface active agents." Use that information to define surfactant in your own words.
2. Summarize the main idea of the text.
3. What can you infer about how effective water without soap or detergent would be in cleaning clothes or hair?
4. Write a letter to a little brother or sister explaining why soap and shampoo are needed when they take a bath. Use very simple terminology.

Rate of Chemical Reaction

Several factors affect how fast a chemical reaction occurs. These factors include concentration, temperature, surface area, pressure, and catalysts.

Complete the graphic organizer by defining and providing an example for each factor that affects the rate of chemical reactions.

concentration

temperature

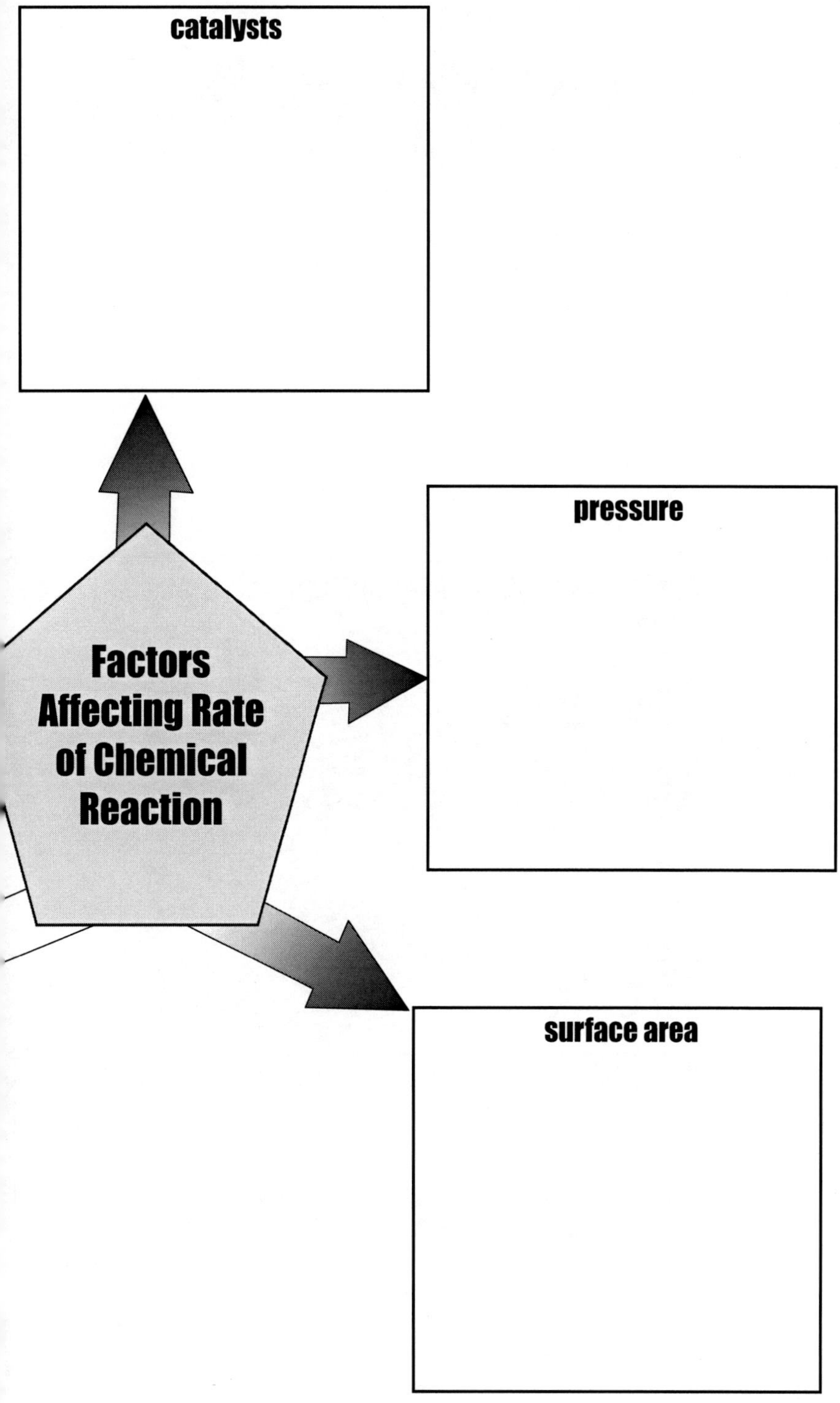
catalysts
pressure
Factors Affecting Rate of Chemical Reaction
surface area

Rocket Launch

Study the text, photograph, and quotes. Then, answer the questions.

One dramatic expression of a chemical reaction is a space shuttle launch. The rockets launching the shuttle use a mixture of liquid hydrogen and liquid oxygen to create an exothermic reaction. The energy produced from the reaction (heat in the form of steam) lifts the 4.5-million-pound vehicle off the ground. Clouds of smoke billow from the bottom of the rockets. Powerful vibrations and thundering noise fill the air.

The shuttle takes only 8.5 minutes to reach space. The energy produced from the chemical reaction allows the vehicle to reach speeds of up to 17,500 miles per hour!

"The vehicle explodes, literally explodes off the pad…the actual liftoff shakes your entire body and soul." –Astronaut Mike McCulley

"Launch is immensely powerful, and you can truly feel yourself in the center of it, like riding an enormous wave, or being pushed and lifted by a huge hand, or shaken in the jaws of a gigantic dog. The vehicle shakes and vibrates, and you are pinned hard down into your seat by the acceleration." –Astronaut Chris Hadfield

PART A: Use the text, picture, and quotes to determine if the statements below are **true** or **false**. Rewrite each false sentence to be true.

1. A space shuttle launch is an example of an endothermic reaction.
2. Liquid hydrogen and liquid oxygen combine to create energy.
3. One sign of a chemical reaction in a rocket launch is the production of heat.
4. The energy produced in a rocket launch moves the rocket very slowly into space.
5. Astronauts feel strong physical effects during a rocket launch.

PART B: Use the text, picture, and quotes to answer the questions.

6. List every sign of a chemical reaction you see in the photograph.
7. Infer why the chemical reaction shown in the photograph would produce heavy vibrations.
8. A. What do the two astronaut quotes have in common?
   B. What physical feelings do the quotes bring to your mind?
9. Find the definition for "simile." Then, explain how the similes in Chris Hadfield's quote contribute to the overall understanding of a rocket launch.

PART C: Make inferences from the text, picture, and quotes to answer the questions.

10. What can you infer about the dangers astronauts face due to the chemical reactions involved in a rocket launch?
11. What do you think Mike McCulley means when he says the rocket launch shakes "your entire body and soul"?
12. Using the information you have gathered from the text, picture, and quotes, write a narrative from the perspective of an astronaut in a rocket launch. Use descriptive words to describe what you see, hear, and feel. Proofread and edit your work.

Catalysts and Enzymes

Read the text and answer the questions.

Catalysts add energy to a chemical reaction. A catalyst can speed up reactions or make reactions stronger. Without a catalyst, some reactions take longer to occur while other reactions can't happen at all. A catalyst is like a burst of energy to help a chemical reaction move forward.

A common example of a chemical catalyst is heat. For instance, if you fill a room with hydrogen gas and oxygen gas, nothing will happen. In order to produce a chemical reaction, you need a catalyst. In this case, the catalyst would be striking a match. With the addition of heat, the room suddenly experiences an explosive chemical reaction where the hydrogen and oxygen gas combine to create water molecules.

Catalysts are also used to carry out functions in the human body. These catalysts are called enzymes. Enzymes live in the cells of the body. There are many different types of enzymes and each has a specific purpose. The correct enzymes allow cells to carry out their functions quickly and effectively.

Sometimes, the human body does not produce the right enzymes to carry out important chemical reactions. A common enzyme deficiency is lactose intolerance. When someone is lactose intolerant, their body does not produce the enzyme lactase. Lactase's job is to break down the lactose, which is the sugar found in milk and dairy products. Without lactase, the body cannot digest lactose and becomes sick. People who suffer from lactose intolerance can take a lactase supplement to help digest dairy products.

1. A. Use a dictionary to define deficiency as it is used in the text. List an antonym.
   B. Use a dictionary to define intolerance as it is used in the text.
2. What role does an enzyme serve in the human body?
3. Write the catalyst in the graphic organizer.

Hydrogen & Oxygen	+		→	H_2O

CONCEPTS AND PROCESSES

Your Body's Metabolism

Read the text and answer the questions.

Metabolism is an essential chemical process for the human body. Metabolism takes the food you eat and turns it into energy you can use.

The process of metabolism is controlled by two organs in your body called the thyroid and pancreas. The thyroid is located in the front of your neck. It produces a chemical called thyroxine. Thyroxine regulates how much energy your body gains from the food you eat. After the thyroxine allows your food to turn to energy, the pancreas, which is located in your abdomen, tells the energy what to do.

Sometimes the body uses the energy to help you complete all your daily activities. Other times, the body stores energy. *Catabolism* occurs when your body uses the energy created from metabolism to complete daily tasks. More specifically, catabolism breaks down carbohydrates, proteins, and fats found in food to produce energy. *Anabolism* is when your body stores energy for later. Anabolism gathers little bundles of carbohydrates, proteins, and fats to be used on days when the body needs extra energy or does not get enough food.

People often experience problems with their metabolism. The most common problems are hypothyroidism and hyperthyroidism. Hypothyroidism is when the thyroid does not produce enough thyroxine to convert food to energy. Hyperthyroidism is when the thyroid produces too much thyroxine and works overtime.

1. Explain how metabolism is a chemical reaction and not a physical reaction.
2. What can you infer about how a healthy and balanced diet affects the body's metabolism?
3. What can you infer about the effects hypothyroidism has on the body? What about hyperthyroidism?
4. Explain why you can eat nothing for a full day and your body will still produce energy. Cite evidence from the text to support your answer.

Chemical Reactions in the Kitchen

Study the chart and answer the questions.

Chemical reactions don't just take place in laboratories. In fact, chemical reactions happen every day in your own home—right in the kitchen! Many of the most common foods we cook involve a chemical reaction. Without chemical reactions, our bread would be flat, our desserts would be dry, and our meat would be less flavorful. Some common examples of chemical reactions in the kitchen are listed here:

Bread

Chemical reactions make the bread we eat soft and airy. Common ingredients that make bread rise are yeast, baking soda, and baking powder. The acid and alkaline in baking powder and soda react to create gas pockets. These pockets fill the dough with air, resulting in fluffy bread. Yeast combines with warm water to <u>ferment</u> the sugars and carbohydrates found in flour. As the sugars ferment, gas bubbles are released into the dough making it rise over time.

Meat

A delicious, grilled steak has undergone a chemical reaction called the Maillard reaction. When you sear meat at a high temperature, the sugars and proteins in meat break down and reconfigure. The effects of this chemical reaction are that the meat browns and emits an earthy smell and juicy flavor.

Meringue

The light, fluffy topping on top of lemon pie and banana pudding is called meringue. This delicious dessert is made from whipping egg whites rapidly with a whisk. During the whipping, air enters the egg whites. The heat from the active whisk causes the amino acid chains in the eggs to unravel. This results in an airy, foamy mix. Sugar is added to hold the delicate mixture together.

Decomposition (Rotting)

All food molds, spoils, or rots eventually. Different chemical reactions occur when food rots. A chemical reaction makes fruits like apples and bananas turn brown when their enzymes combine with oxygen. Other rot is caused by bacteria in food. Over time, the bacteria will release specific enzymes that break down the food for the bacteria to eat. That is why some foods shrink, harden, and disintegrate when left for too long.

1. Use a dictionary to define ferment as it is used in the text.
2. List all signs (heat, odor, gas produced, solid produced, color change) of a chemical reaction in the following:
   A. leavened bread
   B. meat
   C. meringue
   D. rotting food
3. Predict what would happen if a baker forgot to add yeast to his bread. Explain how you came to that conclusion.
4. Work with a partner. Research 5 other chemical reactions that occur in the kitchen. Create a computer presentation to show and describe the chemical reaction in each example.
5. Create a compost pile by collecting any organic remains from cooking in a special, sealed container. Organic remains are any pieces of fruits or vegetables not used in cooking. Watch what happens to the compost pile over time. Explain what chemical reaction is taking place.

PRIMARY SOURCE ANALYSIS

Innovative Life Jacket

A 17-year-old from South Africa has invented a revolutionary life vest with a heat-producing liner. The heat is a product of a chemical reaction between calcium oxide and water. Her invention has the potential to save lives from the threat of <u>*hypothermia*</u> *in frigid water. Below is a paraphrased excerpt from a news article about her invention.*

Read the news article excerpt and answer the questions.

You might be surprised to know that the biggest threat from a boat sinking isn't from the accident itself or from sharks lurking nearby. The biggest threat to a person's life is the loss of body heat from being in cold water too long. Help may be on the way through the work of Danielle Mallabone, a South African teenager. Danielle has invented a liner for life jackets that produces heat through a chemical reaction. Her invention could keep people alive until rescuers arrive.

Mallabone explains that the body's temperature can drop to dangerously low levels even in relatively warm water. She says that is the reason she invented her heat-producing life jacket liner. The liner has pockets that contain a powdered chemical called calcium oxide, which radiates heat when it becomes wet. The heat-producing reaction actually warms up the water between the life jacket and the wearer's body. Mallabone hopes this warmth can fend off hypothermia until the person can be rescued.

How does the chemical reaction work? Heat is generated slowly by the chemical reaction between calcium oxide and water. Mallabone's research found that heat was produced after about 5 minutes. The most intense heat was reached about 25 minutes after the life jacket was immersed in water.

Mallabone's research also shows that the jacket liner will not reach high enough temperatures to risk burns or explosion. No acidic byproducts are produced by the reaction. The liners can also be stored for long periods because calcium oxide doesn't react with everyday humidity in the air.

Original article by Sid Perkins, May 28, 2013, *Student Science*

1. Use the text to infer the meaning of <u>hypothermia</u>. Use a dictionary to check your answer.
2. What type of chemical reaction occurs in Mellabone's jacket?
3. What sign indicates a chemical reaction in the jacket?
4. Create a problem-solution graphic organizer to describe this invention.

Chemical Reactions Vocabulary

Complete the graphic organizer for each vocabulary word below.

catalyst	endothermic	precipitate
chemical equation	enzyme	product
chemical reaction	exothermic	reactant

DEFINITION

FACTS/CHARACTERISTICS

WORD

USE IT IN A SENTENCE

Chemical Reactions Hands-On

Perform the experiments with the supervision of a teacher or parent and complete the lab report for each one.

Balloon Blow-up

Supplies: an empty, clean bottle, vinegar, baking soda, balloon, funnel

Step 1: Use the funnel to pour 2 tablespoons of baking soda in the balloon.

Step 2: Fill the bottle halfway with vinegar.

Step 3: Stretch the balloon over the top of the open bottle. Be careful not to let the baking soda and vinegar mix.

Step 4: Predict what will happen to the balloon on the lab report.

Step 5: Tip the balloon so that the baking soda flows into the vinegar. Be sure to hold the top of the balloon during this process.

Step 6: Observe and record your findings.

Elephant Toothpaste

Supplies: an empty plastic 16 oz bottle, ½ cup hydrogen peroxide, 1 pkg yeast, ¼ cup warm water, dish soap, a cup, food coloring (optional)

Step 1: Pour peroxide into 16 oz bottle. Have an adult complete this step.

Step 2: Place 3-5 drops of food coloring into the peroxide.

Step 3: Add a squirt of dish soap. Swirl the bottle to mix.

Step 4: In a separate cup, combine yeast and warm water, stir to combine.

Step 5: Predict what will happen when the mixtures combine on the lab report.

Step 6: Pour the yeast mixture into the peroxide mixture.

Step 7: Observe and record your findings.

Lab Report

Name ______________________________

Question ______________________________

____

Prediction ______________________________

____

Materials

Procedure

Results and Conclusions ______________________________

____

____

____

Correlations to Common Core State Standards

For your convenience, correlations are listed page-by-page and for the entire book!

This book is correlated to the Common Core State Standards for English Language Arts grades 3-8, and to Common Core State Standards for Literacy in History, Science, & Technological Subjects grades 6-8.

Correlations are highlighted in gray.

PAGE #	READING *Includes:* RI: Reading Informational Text RH: Reading History	WRITING *Includes:* W: Writing WHST: Writing History, Science, & Technology	LANGUAGE *Includes:* L: Language LF: Language Foundational Skills	SPEAKING & LISTENING *Includes:* SL: Speaking & Listening
2	RI RH . **1** **2** 3 4 5 6 7 **8** 9 **10**	W WHST . 1 **2** 3 **4** 5 6 **7** **8** 9 **10**	L LF . 1 2 3 4 5 **6**	SL . **1** 2 3 **4** 5 **6**
3	RI RH . **1** 2 **3** **4** 5 6 7 8 9 **10**	W WHST . 1 **2** 3 **4** 5 6 7 **8** 9 10	L LF . 1 2 3 **4** **5** **6**	SL . **1** 2 3 4 5 6
4-5	RI RH . **1** 2 **3** **4** 5 6 **7** 8 9 **10**	W WHST . **1** **2** 3 **4** 5 6 **7** 8 9 10	L LF . 1 2 3 4 5 6	SL . 1 2 3 4 5 6
6	RI RH . **1** **2** **3** **4** **5** 6 7 8 9 **10**	W WHST . 1 **2** 3 **4** 5 6 **7** **8** **9** **10**	L LF . 1 2 3 **4** 5 **6**	SL . **1** 2 3 **4** 5 **6**
7	RI RH . 1 2 **3** 4 5 6 **7** 8 9 10	W WHST . 1 **2** 3 **4** 5 6 **7** **8** **9** **10**	L LF . 1 2 3 **4** 5 **6**	SL . 1 2 3 4 5 6
8-9	RI RH . **1** **2** **3** 4 5 **6** 7 **8** **9** **10**	W WHST . 1 **2** 3 **4** 5 6 7 **8** **9** **10**	L LF . 1 2 3 **4** 5 **6**	SL . 1 2 3 4 5 6
10	RI RH . **1** 2 **3** **4** 5 6 **7** 8 9 **10**	W WHST . 1 **2** 3 **4** 5 6 **7** 8 9 **10**	L LF . 1 2 3 **4** **5** **6**	SL . 1 2 3 4 5 6
11	RI RH . **1** **2** **3** **4** **5** 6 7 8 9 **10**	W WHST . 1 **2** 3 **4** 5 6 7 **8** 9 **10**	L LF . 1 2 3 **4** 5 **6**	SL . 1 2 3 4 5 6
12-13	RI RH . **1** 2 3 **4** 5 6 **7** 8 9 **10**	W WHST . 1 **2** 3 **4** 5 6 **7** **8** 9 **10**	L LF . 1 2 3 **4** 5 **6**	SL . 1 2 3 4 5 6
14-15	RI RH . **1** **2** **3** **4** 5 **6** **7** 8 **9** **10**	W WHST . 1 **2** **3** **4** 5 6 7 **8** **9** **10**	L LF . 1 2 3 **4** **5** **6**	SL . 1 2 3 4 5 6
16	RI RH . **1** **2** **3** **4** 5 6 **7** 8 9 **10**	W WHST . 1 **2** 3 **4** 5 6 7 8 9 **10**	L LF . 1 2 3 **4** **5** **6**	SL . 1 2 3 4 5 6
17	RI RH . **1** 2 **3** **4** 5 6 7 **8** 9 **10**	W WHST . 1 **2** 3 **4** 5 6 7 **8** **9** **10**	L LF . 1 2 3 **4** **5** **6**	SL . 1 2 3 4 5 6
18-19	RI RH . **1** 2 **3** **4** 5 6 **7** **8** 9 **10**	W WHST . 1 **2** 3 **4** 5 **6** **7** **8** **9** **10**	L LF . 1 2 3 **4** 5 **6**	SL . 1 2 3 4 5 6
20	RI RH . **1** **2** **3** **4** **5** 6 7 8 9 **10**	W WHST . 1 **2** 3 **4** 5 6 7 8 **9** **10**	L LF . 1 2 3 **4** 5 **6**	SL . 1 2 3 4 5 6
21	RI RH . 1 2 3 **4** 5 6 7 8 9 **10**	W WHST . 1 2 3 **4** 5 6 7 8 9 10	L LF . 1 2 3 **4** 5 **6**	SL . 1 2 3 4 5 6
22-23	RI RH . **1** **2** **3** 4 **5** 6 7 8 9 **10**	W WHST . 1 **2** 3 **4** 5 6 7 8 **9** **10**	L LF . 1 2 3 4 5 6	SL . 1 2 3 4 5 6
COMPLETE BOOK	RI RH . **1** **2** **3** **4** **5** **6** **7** **8** **9** **10**	W WHST . **1** **2** **3** **4** **5** **6** **7** **8** **9** **10**	L LF . 1 2 3 **4** **5** **6**	SL . **1** **2** 3 **4** **5** **6**

For the complete Common Core standard identifier, combine your grade + "." + letter code above + "." + number code above.

In addition to the correlations indicated here, the activities may be adapted or expanded to align to additional standards and to meet the diverse needs of your unique students!